Gratitude, Faith, and Humor Will Get You Through Your Disappointments

"What if" Promotes Fear.
"Even if" Promotes Faith.

Edward L. Roth, CFP®

Dedication

The Purpose and goal of writing this book is to be a source of encouragement to my children, grandchildren, and great-grandchildren and dedicate it to my wife and partner of these past 66 years. Without her loving support, it would have been impossible to have the rewarding life that I have lived. This book is dedicated to Mildred L Bontrager Roth, who is the love of my life.

Registered Principal

Raymond James Financial Services, Inc.

Member FINRA/SIPC phone: 419-446-2701 fax: 419-445-3607 103 Main Street

P.O. Box 53129

Pettisville, OH 43553-0129

Edward.Roth@Raymondjames.com

Acknowledgment

A special thank you to Steve Parker and his team for their professional help in creating this book. They are the greatest writing couches a person can have. If you have an idea for a book, it is my recommendation you consult with Steve Parker and her team.

Edward L. Roth, CFP®

Registered Principal

Raymond James Financial Services, Inc.

Member FINRA/SIPC phone: 419-446-2701 fax: 419-445-3607 103 Main Street

P.O. Box 53129

Pettisville, OH 43553-0129

Edward.Roth@Raymondjames.com

About the Author

My parents, Reuben and Norma Roth started their married life on January 26, 1928, in Milford, Nebraska. They moved that year to Alberta, Canada, and homesteaded on the prairie in Western Alberta. I remember my father telling me that the first building they built was a granary because they wanted to make sure they had storage for the grain harvest in the fall. So they lived in the granary until the house was built. That is where I learned about hard work and core values.

In 1941, my family moved to Northwest Ohio to establish a life in the USA. My first business experience was a Newspaper route at age 10. From a very young age, I was taught that a person must be independent and resourceful enough to be in business for himself. I quickly learned that not everyone pays on time.

This book is sharing what some of my failures were and how those failures were a stepping stone in my life. It is through failures that we learn to be successful. For every adversity, there is a seed of an equivalent or greater benefit. It is my goal to help the readers understand the truth of life that will help them have a more meaningful life and to learn from some of the hard lessons of life. There will always be the calm before the storm or the storm that comes after the calm in our lives. However, if we have no rain, we would soon live in a desert.

"The greater danger for most of us lies not in setting our aim too high and falling short; but in setting our aim too low, and achieving our mark."
– Michelangel

Preface

In a world full of competitors, become a successful person. The meaning of success may vary from person to person depending on a lot of factors. Success is not just about becoming a millionaire or doing whatever it takes to get rich. Sometimes success is all about having a roof over your head and not having a thing to worry about at all. Or it is becoming a helping hand that can guide others when they are lost.

This world is not as complicated as people make it out to be. Some of the complications we see prevailing in this world are due to our actions and nothing more. Our actions come with consequences, and some of these consequences can prove to be fatal for us. I am writing this book to help people simplify their complicated lives and help them understand that success is not the only thing we need to strive for in this world. We need to strive for a better version of ourselves with every step we take in this world.

Most of all, enjoy yourself.

Contents

Page Left Blank Intentionally

Chapter 1: Gratitude

"You will be enriched in every way to be generous in every way, which through us will produce thanksgiving to God." -Corinthians 9:11

"You will be enriched in every way to be generous in every way, which through us will produce thanksgiving to God." -Corinthians 9:11

God has given each of us our share of blessings: food, shelter, family, love, and friendship, to name a few. Even those among us who seem less privileged are blessed in some way or the other. They might know how to seek happiness in the small pleasures of life. Although it is not everything you see, it is unique to that person.

The simplicity and complexity of life and its experiences are beyond the comprehension of man. All too often, we run out of the last piece of candy in the jar or munch on the last cookie ourselves, only to then look skywards and complain to God: "Why me?!" But we are also the ones who ate the food God gave us! We are the ones who were chosen to be provided with the best and sweetest things in life when we, mortal humans, did not do much to deserve them. It is only through the benevolence of the Almighty that we get food in abundance.

So how should we react when the cookie jar becomes empty, you ask? We do it by taking the last bite, looking skywards, and saying, "Thank you, God, for all you have given me."

If instead, you choose to cry and complain about things you don't have, then you won't be able to explore any opportunity that comes your way. For instance, walking barefoot in the dirt with no shoes on would allow you to go looking for the right pair of shoes. But if you are not optimistic or do not show gratitude, it will only make your time ten times worse, and all you would be able to think about are the negative things. On the other hand, if you practice gratitude and thank God for the clothes he has given you to cover your body and other blessings, you would be able to come up with ideas to help you get out of the situation. And if not, you would at least be able to appreciate the clear sky above you or come to feel empathy for those like you who walk in the dirt barefoot every day. To put it simply, it is important always to be grateful to the Almighty for whatever little you have. You are filled with unhappiness by not doing it, but by showing gratitude, you become thankful and happy.

Gratitude is not just an attitude; it is a way of life. By adopting it, you not only accept your good luck in receiving what you have received but also show humility and express the acceptance of the fact that if at any point, you lose possession of what you own right now, you would know that it has been taken from you for the same reason it was given to you; you do not know or fully understand that reason, but you know that God trusts you enough to put you through a difficult test.

It is a way of life in another sense: it makes you empathize with the people around you who have just as much as you, or even less than you. You see people more clearly and understand their actions better than before. You basically look into their empty cookie jar and go, "Hey! I have a similar-looking one! This only means that we can fill it up with better-baked cookies now! How cool is that?" and maybe give them a high-five. (Make sure you know them well enough to do that; giving high-fives to strangers and formal acquaintances is not recommended).

Gratitude is a Basic Need

Like breathing, eating, drinking and sleeping are our basic needs in life, so is practicing gratitude. The only difference is that not everyone is consciously aware of it. We cannot simply go about life consuming the gifts of God without ever feeling like we are some of the luckiest ones out there to have deserved this. If you have ever felt this, I say congratulations! You know and understand the highs and lows of life better than others.

In this day and age, where faith is dwindling amongst people and is being replaced with pride, it is of utmost importance to remember your roots and say thanks to those who helped you develop and groom into who you have become today.

Therefore, since we are receiving a kingdom that cannot be shaken, let us be thankful, and so worship God acceptably with reverence and awe, **Hebrews 12:28**

If life is a meal that you are excited to get your hands on and devour, then gratitude is like cutlery; it is a basic need you cannot go without. Your attempts to try without it would only create a mess, and you would not be able to keep your hands clean and your heart satisfied if you do not have it. What good is such a meal that does not give your heart pleasure and peace but only partially satisfies your animalistic hunger? No good, I say.

The need to practice gratitude is higher in our world than in any other epoch now, more than ever. As humans, we have gotten too comfortable in our skins to the point of blaming another for our loss and ourselves and our egos for gain; we stomp our feet like children when our toys are taken from us and jump, and dance like them give back. The element of gratitude makes us mature.

Besides giving us a path to work on in life, gratitude gives us opportunities and opens window opportunities for us when we start giving up on life. It gives us hope during the dark, troubled times and makes us empathize with our fellow beings and ensures that we have enough strength to move forward towards glory.

How to Be Grateful

It is essential, it is essential, and it is the need of the time, but how does one practice gratitude?

The simplest way to do it is to feel in hearts of hearts that it is not and was not in your power to reach where you have and received what you have achieved. To submit to the Almighty's power and accept that you are a small being in front of Him will eventually compel you to show gratitude.

Being grateful does not always mean saying "Thank you" to everyone all the time. It is not like you have to kiss the hands of the chef who cooked a good meal for you or constantly nag the person who lent you a few pennies just to show him your good side. No! It is a feeling that manifests itself into action when it is fully internalized, and it is not limited to people and things. Its spectrum is way broader than just material things; it extends to relationships, nature, emotions like love, happiness, sadness, tangible or intangible, big or small, abstract or concrete.

One has to feel gratitude fully. It is to trust the power of the Almighty fully. It is a greater power outside of you and away from your reach that makes you and helps you do it. This humble realization and its internalization to the core of your being begins your journey of practicing gratitude. Only after knowing that you cannot do anything do you begin to do anything at all.

Moreover, the way to be grateful is not to feel thankful only when life gives you the best for your efforts and hard work. You must stay grateful even when you do not get what you desire. Wherever the tide takes you, you hold on to your boat and keep it steady whether you face a storm or the sun shines bright at you.

Grateful is Successful

And whatever you do, whether in word or deed, do it all in the name of the Lord Jesus, giving thanks to God the Father through him. **Colossians 3:17**

With an attitude that is not bitter towards any hardship or downfall, any grateful person is bound to be successful in many walks of life. For different people, success is defined differently. Whether it is financial, familial, personal, or any other kind, feeling comfortable in and seeing the reason behind an unsuccessful experience will ultimately make that person work harder and more honestly than anyone who only blames life and the God above for putting him in a bad place. Life is like a box of chocolates, but you may not always get the chocolate you like the most, but being patient on getting the okay and not-so-okay ones will guarantee your chances of getting the best one sooner or later.

Disappointments are unavoidable. We are born pure, but our journey from being a child to becoming a mature adult is bound to corrupt our personalities and ways despite our trying our hardest to keep clean. One way or another, life will find a way to bring you down. But while it does that, it will also provide you with tools to fight it back. And one of the strongest and sturdiest tools you will find is gratitude. While it empties your cookie jar, it gives you the unique opportunity of filling it up with whatever you want.

When you are set on the path of trying again and trying harder to fix what was broken, that endeavor alone will bring success. The act of fixing something broken is a form of success in itself. Therefore, try to lead your life with gratitude.

Be grateful! It cannot be put any more simply or accurately. Forget all the complexities and immerse yourself in gratitude; all the other emotions will follow. You will find love, happiness, and peace, which will take away the pain and worries life will throw at you. Gratitude is linked to every pleasant emotion in a chain that cannot be broken in any way, as long as the person holding it has a strong grip.

Be thankful! The hair you have on your head, the skin to protect you from diseases, the hands to hold the blessings God has sent, and the feet to walk on the earth with pride are all factors anyone and every one of us should be grateful for. Moving on, count the blessings that are unique to you and bow your head down to let Him know that you see it all. It is a matter of acknowledgment and servitude, after all.

Every successful person you have ever come across in life was once grateful for whatever little he had and is now grateful for the added blessings.

Be grateful for every breath you draw, every muscle you move, every color you see, and every second you spend. Begin from the smallest of things, and God will give you bigger reasons. The ant starts from the bottom of the hill makes its way through the bumps and craters only to reach the top untouched. If anything, it finds sustenance there. The world is your hill, God, your provider, and there is much on the hill to be grateful for.

Thoughts to Ponder

- Have an Attitude of Gratitude! It will gravitate people to you.
- It is much more rewarding to be a cheerleader than a critic.
- A forced smile is much better than a sincere frown.
- Be thankful for the good and the bad!

Chapter 2: Be Humble

While being grateful for everything you do have, you also ought to be humble in the matters in which you do not have prosperity and success, only by knowing in your heart that you can only do so much with your hands and your feet that you gain what is outside of the realm of your active actions.

Humble yourselves before the Lord, and he will lift you up. **James 4:10**

We are too small for the might of providence, and the world we live in can sometimes be too big for us. While it is good to know where you are going and have confidence in your journey, it is essential that you do not let your confidence turn into arrogance. Accept having limited knowledge of the universe, and it will constantly teach you newer things. Socrates, the great Greek philosopher, always said that the only thing he knew was that he knew nothing. Yet, history shows that he was probably the only man who knew a lot more than those that came after him. His humility was the beginning as well as the result of his journey towards truth. So, dear readers, if you wish to achieve something in life and be successful—in ways more than one—then adopt humility in your attitude. If you want happiness, love, bliss, and everything nice, be humble, and everything else will follow.

Humility is the fear of the Lord;

its wages are riches and honor and life. **Proverbs 22:4**

It is Important

Our thinking processes define our actions. Everything we do is defined by an ideology that pushed us to perform that action. And, that action, in turn, comes to define our character and who we are as a person. Patterns of habits form a personality. To put it simply, what and how we think ultimately makes us who we are. So, if we think in a dark, spiteful,

7

condemning, and repulsive manner, the person we will eventually come to be would be of the same kind. But, if we are kind, generous, pious, and humble, the kind of persons we will become will be the same. To be righteous, one needs to think and act righteously.

While it is important that we take care of who we are becoming as people through our actions, it is also important to be humble because life is often out of hand. As mortal humans, a lot of things will happen or have happened that are or were not under our control. As said above, this world can sometimes prove to be too big for our small hands. Although we cannot do much about taking control, we can behave in a manner that the mighty hand of nature and God are lenient on us. If we cannot control our fate, we can, at least, show humility by submitting to it.

What scares us is really only what we do not fully understand. It is fine not to understand everything and be scared: it is a lesson in humility. By knowing that we do not hold the world in our hands and being humble, we move faster on the journey of learning. Moreover, our attitude towards the things we do have certain knowledge about becomes more positive.

Mark Twain once said:

It ain't those parts of the Bible that I can't understand that bother me; it is the parts that I do understand.

If this tells us anything, it is this: not knowing is not as bad as knowing and being unable to process it. Thus, being humble teaches us more and makes us see deeper meanings in the things we do already know.

We NEED to be Humble

There is a need for us to remain humble because that way, we keep challenging ourselves. It is important to be humble, but more than that, it is important that we stay humble. We must always ask ourselves: what are we even doing with our lives if we do not grow by taking on newer opportunities for ourselves to learn from and spreading them around us to those who need them more than us?

"The greater danger for most of us lies not in setting our aim too high and falling short, but in setting our aim too low and achieving our mark."

The great artist Michelangelo said this. He knew that the mark of excellence is not what one is able to create but how intensely one challenges himself and tries to fulfill it. That mark of excellence is found in those who are humble. When we have accepted that the circumstances in our life are out of our control, we become brave in a manner unknown to the herd. There is a kind of power achieved by giving in to powers greater than you; the strength that comes with submission makes us rise higher. We can aim higher than we ever did and achieve goals we never even dared to set.

Do not, for a moment, think that by putting us in difficult times is God punishing us. He is only doing it so he can be with us throughout the process of getting out of the adversaries. God merely tries to get the attention of mortals by putting them through what seems like challenges; look at these little reminders like blessings for which you were chosen. The author CS Lewis beautifully explains this phenomenon:

Pain insists upon being attended to. God whispers to us in our pleasures, speaks in our consciences, but shouts in our pains. It is his megaphone to rouse a deaf world."

Just like gratitude makes you see and feel things more clearly than before, humility does the same. Being happy with what you have been blessed with and being humble about the same are ways to ask God to give you more so you can spread the blessings and share them with those around you. If you are humble, you will be sensitive enough to see and know who has what and how much more they deserve from life. You eventually become the source of blessings for others.

Being humble empowers you and those around you. It is a form of positivity that keeps spreading with every action one takes. It is an attitude that defines our lifestyles. All of us *need* to be humble to be better, braver, and smarter versions of ourselves. Being a source of comfort for our loved ones is a bonus point. Money comes and goes but, is personal growth, not the kind of success that really matters?

Who is wise and understanding among you? Let them show it by their good life, by deeds done in the humility that comes from wisdom. **James 3:13**

The Lessons It Teaches Us

A humble attitude takes a person a long way into life, for it teaches us valuable lessons. Staying humble mostly means knowing that life is unpredictable and that the next move it plays on us could decide our fate. It means that we stay prepared to throw our weapons when it is time and loosen our grip on the ropes of success and glory because some things are supposed to come to us on their own. Being humble means knowing when to stop trying; it gives us the power to tell when providence wants something from us. These lessons that it teaches are not picked up by all who try but come to those who truly practice humility.

Being humble also teaches us that the road to success is always under construction. There is not a single spot called "success" where you can drive your car and leave it parked for the rest of eternity. It does not work like that. If it did, all of us would be successful. The definition of success is elusive and left for us to define. For most, it means earning big amounts of money. That is not the right definition for a truly fulfilling life. If anything, it makes the man greedy and ever wanting more. It is the only currency that does not really get anyone anything despite it seeming like the opposite. For a person to be successful, they need to ask themselves what the one thing that they want the most is? What is it that truly makes them happy? If it is something that they cannot run after to the finish line, it is noble and can be attained by staying humble. If it is the opposite, then the person would run away from humility into the claws of greed and hubris. The person will speak for attention and not for his genuine intention.

He has shown you, O mortal, what is good.

And what does the Lord require of you?

To act justly and to love mercy

and to walk humbly with your God. **Micah 6:8**

Make the Decision

Then he said to them, "Whoever welcomes this little child in my name welcomes me, and whoever welcomes me welcomes the one who sent me. For it is the one who is least among you all who is the greatest." **Luke 9:48**

In the eyes of the Almighty, the least is the greatest. He who has naught is rich with feeling and humility, for he understands the paradox of having everything while not *having* anything. The simplicity is in poverty — that is monetary poverty, for the spirit can be rich no matter how less a man owns cash—is nothing like the worries of richness. So, being able will provide you with valuable lessons in life *and* make you rich in an unconventional way (It might even mean in a conventional way, but what would a humble man care?). The choice is yours.

If my people, who are called by my name, will humble themselves and pray and seek my face and turn from their wicked ways, then I will hear from heaven, and I will forgive their sin and will heal their land. **2 Chronicles 7:14**

Humbling oneself also means being open to listening to others. Facts are spineless in this day and age, where things are changing in a matter of seconds. He who keeps an open mind will go a long way while the stubborn man will suffer uncountable miseries. The power to keep your own opinion aside to consider another person's is rare, but the humble man owns it with all the other powers he has. You can either choose to stand steadfast in your place while the world moves or choose to move while the world stays stationary. The Sun stands, and the Earth revolves; who do we know to be alive and housing the whole of humanity? You know the answer – the choice is yours.

Moreover, circumstances in life do not always allow a person to be sure about things he was previously sure about. No one would have the energy, either, to do anything if they did not have worries in life. While stress and tension may be considered bad things in the modern world, they also determine who we are and how humble we choose to be. It is up to us to make the stumbling stones in life into stepping stones. You can either keep staring at the stones, waiting for them to magically disappear, or humble yourself and enjoy the presence. The choice is yours.

God gives us hardships to test our patience, and by staying humble in the face of those hardships, we prove to him to be His true servants. The responsibility of handling the hardship like a true follower is on our shoulders. You can either fight against the will of God or accept what He gives and stay humble despite it. The choice, dear reader, is always yours.

Therefore, as God's chosen people, holy and dearly loved, clothe yourselves with compassion, kindness, humility, gentleness, and patience. **Colossians 3:12**

Thoughts to Ponder

- For every adversity, there is an equivalent or greater benefit.
- Keep looking ahead for all the good that is to come.
- Climb the mountain to see the world, not for the world to see you.

Chapter 3: Humor

Life makes sure to give every one of us a good amount of lemons, and while we can make lemonade out of them, we can also juggle them away! It is all about perspective. You can either sulk in your adversities or decorate them to make showpieces! Life should not be taken more seriously than it needs to. A little humor in every situation is necessary if you want to get through difficult times with calm nerves.

Why is it Important to Laugh?

Humor is important because 1) it makes you see the brighter side of the picture and take your attention away from the darkness for a good while, 2) it refreshes your mind enough to come up with effective ways to deal with what has gone wrong; the happy chemicals move you up on your feet into taking action and 3) generally, it lengthens your life as it stops you from taking all the burden of everything on your shoulders.

It is no news that we suffer losses and live through pain in the general course of our lives. It happens to everyone every day and is the way of the world. When there is spring in gardens, there is autumn too. Loss and gain, sadness and happiness, lows and highs are all co-existing in life with each other. There is a portion of each written in the fate of all of us. The purpose of repeating this fact is to establish that hardships and difficulties are inevitable. Murphy's Law states that what can go wrong will go wrong. But while Murphy said that, the German poet Rainer Maria Rilke also presented the idea that whatever we receive from life from the outside of our beings is constant. He presented the metaphor of our circumstances being like the Sun, stationery in its place, always the same, and just as strong as the previous day. But we, humans, are like the planet Earth that revolves around the Sun. We keep moving no matter what. The changes we experience are going to come at us until we cease to be, but we have the power to take them on with the same standing. He says: *"The future stands firm ... but we move in infinite space."*

So, there is one way of dealing with the 'firm' output of the future: staying our ground with the strongest weapon we have: humor.

When we choose to take a matter lightly in the sense that we do not let it take over our whole being, we are giving ourselves space and resources to deal with it. When we breathe deep and relax and make a good old joke about it, we are better prepared to solve and resolve the issue than we would be if we worried about it like it was the end of the world. By smiling and laughing, we train our brains to generate happy chemicals. Serotonin and dopamine are chemicals in our brain that make us feel happiness and pleasure. Sometimes, they are a little difficult and shy to come out. So we have to take things into our own hands and lure them out with a crispy smile and a positive attitude.

When these chemicals flush into our brain and body, they make our system go at a healthy speed, like a racing car speeding up on special fluids! So, to keep their supply steady, it is crucial that we remember to take things on a lighter note instead of being serious about them more than we need to be.

Furthermore, it has been scientifically proven that adding a little humor to your life makes you live longer and healthier. The Scientific American says that "Women with a strong sense of humor were found to live longer despite illness, especially cardiovascular disease and infection. Mirthful men seem to be protected against infection." If you are miserable, of course, you would not want to lengthen the span of that experience. But merriment learns from itself. It knows that the people who are merry like being so, and so it ensures a longer period of time for them in this merry world. So crack your best joke and keep going!

At All Times, At All Cost!

Keeping a humorous touch in life is not all about having a good time; it effectively improves the quality of your experiences. Life can be difficult, and to have enough to look forward to the next day is a blessing in itself. Sometimes, you have to give yourself that blessing when no one or nothing else does. During tough times, it is the boat that keeps you on the surface and eventually takes you to the shore. Without it, you are all but immersed in the darkness under the ocean.

"Humor is perhaps a sense of intellectual perspective: an awareness that some things are really important, others not; and that the two kinds are most oddly jumbled in everyday affairs." –Christopher Morley

Sometimes, it is better to force a smile than to sincerely frown. Honesty may be the best virtue, but the mind needs to be tricked sometimes. Feel the reason for the frown that is forcing to show itself on your face alright; feel it to the full. But when it comes to presenting yourself to the world, shift your mood for them like a magician. Pain and sadness will thrive no matter what; what we can do is be positive about how we get affected by them. We can choose to be or not be affected by a calamity. Surely, process your emotions in a healthy way, but do not let them consume your whole being. A fake smile becomes a real one in no time, but an actual frown takes ages to be undone.

Tough times present opportunities to a man. He can either be crushed down under the weight of their nature or fight them head-on and maintain his composure. While strong men also give up and feel pain from time to time, it is their mark to also suffer through it quietly, instead of making a show. What putting up a smile instead of a frown does is that it teaches you a lesson in strength and perseverance. Despite all that keeps happening, you and your attitude stay the same. You do not lose perspective and keep believing in yourself to stand firm in the face of however many adversities that come your way.

Faking a smile is not being dishonest, it is merely trying your best to fight a good fight. It is a weapon in warfare, a tool to mend what is broken from the outside. Humor has power, and it is always in our hands to unleash it.

The Book Endorses Humor

Then our mouth was filled with laughter, and our tongue with shouts of joy; then they said among the nations, "The Lord has done great things for them." Psalm 126:2

It is a sign of being grateful to God and saying thanks for His grace and blessings. Laughter and enjoyment show that He has given us enough to not be lost in the labyrinth of that which is out of our hands to attain. It is a sign that He has chosen us to be away from the sin of greed by being content with what we rightly own. He wants us to laugh and rejoice in the face of everything good and bad to let Him know that we see and accept His grace with all our being. So by keeping a humorous touch in all our dealings, we are not only doing ourselves a favor but also keeping the Almighty pleased.

All the days of the afflicted are evil, but the cheerful of heart has a continual feast. Proverbs 15:15

They say that the more we tell ourselves, "It's cold," the colder we are going to feel. The more attention we pay to a thing, the more it pays attention to us and shows itself. So, the more we feel the infliction of pain and sadness in life, the more it is going to take us in its arms. But if we choose to pay heed to lighter, better things in life, they will pay heed to us and make our circumstances better.

Humor is a crucial ingredient in the recipe for a prosperous and accomplished life. Without it, the dish is just bland and tasteless. In times like these, when there are a hundred things to crush your spirit, show some strength by putting on a smile.

A joyful heart is good medicine, but a crushed spirit dries up the bones.
Proverbs 17:22

Thoughts to Ponder

- It takes 17 muscles to smile but 42 to frown. Rest up.

- As you age, try and have a twinkle in your wrinkle!

- Humor is the most effective way of communication.

- Laughter is the language the northerners *and* the southerners understand.

Chapter 4: Family

*"Family is not an important thing. It's everything.–**Michael J. Fox***

Man is a social being. His interaction with the world begins with the house he grows up in and the people around him in the form of family. It is the first unit of people, the first tribe, that he belongs to. Family forms the basis and foundation of his personality; their traditions, customs, rituals, habits, and ways of life are adopted by the young one who continues to perpetuate them further in his own life. Besides contributing to his life, his family supports him and helps him become the person he is destined to be.

Blood is thicker than water. The bond formed among a few people is far from superficial; it grows to become as strong as a chain of many links that will not come apart no matter how much it is pulled from both ends. The members of one family suffer adversities together and provide all kinds of support, etching in their natures an eternal concern and consideration for one another. Such a bond is not only hard to find in other aspects of life, but it is also the kind that makes one have some hope in life when everything else seems dark and devoid of any light.

We *Need* Family

Even before modern psychology proved the essential role of a strong familial bond at home in the life, health, and stability of an individual, it was understood that man's life begins at home and ends at home. Wherever he might go, he leaves his home in the morning and returns there at night. However much the world may progress if one does not have a place of comfort to turn to when he needs it the most, the progress will not do any good. The idea and satisfaction of knowing that people are waiting for us back home and are praying for our safety make every experience away from them worth the input and hard work.

"The family is the first essential cell of human society." –Pope John XXIII

The individualistic view of life as seen in this day and age may be liberating for some, but it is only harming their mental states and physical well-being. We *need* family. Even if you choose to live away from them to make a life of your own, you must keep your connection with them. The point is that if you forget them, you forget your roots. The man who forgets where he came from loses sight of his future, too, without even realizing it. Only when he suffers the last blow from a lonely and dry life will he understand what he had done. By then, it is too late.

It does not have to be like that. The only thing one has to remember to keep the connection with his family alive is that love is the basis of everything in this world. The gratitude and humor that he so wishes to adopt in his life will not mean anything if he cannot give a small amount of his time to the people he grew up around. Indeed, the family can be brutal sometimes. But working through those difficulties and coming to terms with the different behaviors to stand on the shared ground is the work put in that makes the fruit sweet.

There is nothing weak about needing people. We depend on one another for survival, and we always have. If anything, it is this dependence that makes life beautiful. While you cannot live a wholly detached life, there are also people out there who need your love and support to keep going. We all make a difference in one another's lives; one brick supports another and creates a strong structure. Think of standing alone, and you are in pieces before you even know it. So keep your loved ones close and cherish the moments with them because you *need* their love.

Legacy and Posterity

"Our legacy is how we spend our time and who we spend it with." - Jim Stengel

Besides providing love and support to a child, a family instills in him the values that make him a good person. It is a cruel world, and it is easy to be led astray; many people are there to make that happen, while only a few would help you walk the right path. Family is made of such people. They teach the child the difference between right and wrong and make him see what is good and what is bad. It sounds like a simple and easy concept, but the task of teaching that to someone who does not understand how the world works is one of the most difficult things to do in the world.

Too many children are ignored and left to learn independently; the concepts of good and bad and the line between them blurred make them get involved in harmful habits. They end up making bad decisions that affect their lives in the long run. The absence of family on their heads, someone to tell them which way to go from the crossroads, dooms them forever. With a family present, the fate of a child does not suffer. Even though not all of us get to be a part of a family, some people do not value their families. They make a terrible mistake by pushing away that kind of unconditional love.

Our parents' and elders' teachings decorate our lives and make us prosper. By simply holding certain values in us, we do the world around us a favor. The actions we take and the interactions we make, we slowly dissipate and spread those values to the people and auras around us. By choosing not to act with violence, we teach the spectators that it is not the better way; it is not a virtue. Our actions make many people wonder about the ideologies behind them and make them adopt them. By simply being and applying the values passed on to us by our parents, we make the world a better place. We pass on their legacy and our legacy by walking in our family's footsteps.

Another way we maintain the legacy of our family by passing on the same teachings of love, kindness, empathy, compassion, faith, gratitude, and more to our children. Legacy is not limited to the amount of money we leave in our wills for our children or the pieces of property; it is the nature we leave them with. The lessons, the experiences, the love shared, and the love felt is what continue our existence in this world even after we have long passed. The memories we leave behind with our loved ones keep us alive as long as they are alive and the ones that come after them.

By being kind to your family, you ensure a lifetime's worth of return of that same kindness. By loving your family, you are writing your will to be in the world forever, despite physical absence.

Love your family and let them love you, and you will live forever.

In Time of Test, Family is Best

"In time of test, family is best." –Burmese Proverb

Blood is thicker than water because it can feel the pain and throbs flowing through another's body. A family is a unit, just like the human body. If one part of our body, such as our ankle, is hurting, the whole body from tip to toe feels that pain and works towards curing it. It is a single system that does everything in its power to get back to normal. Likewise, when you are hurting, so are your mother, father, and siblings. If you are lucky, there may be more people in your family like grandparents, uncles, aunts, and cousins who feel for you like you are their immediate family. These people look out for you in difficult times and celebrate the good ones with you.

As we move on in life, we see a whole lot of tricky situations. Sometimes, all we need is a little push and a little support to continue on that path, whether it is a business you are trying to set up or a family feud you wish to resolve or survive through. At these times, these family members who look out for us provide that push in the form of financial help or a shoulder lean on. When all our friends are busy, we find our family waiting to be asked for help. In sickness, illness, and other dreary situations, when life seems too heavy to be borne, it is our family who never walks away.

When life is moving upwards for us, when we reach milestones and achieve great things, it is also a family that feels pride in us and wishes us even better luck for further future endeavors. They celebrate our first steps, our first word, our first day of school, our first friendship, our first victory, and everything else that comes along. When we grow up and are walking on our own feet, they still cheer from behind. Graduation, getting a job, achieving success, getting married, and having children are milestones through which we find them standing by our side. And when it comes to starting our own family, we replicate their support and give our children everything we received.

In a nutshell, no matter what we do or where we go in life, our family is there to help. What we can and should do is never prove ourselves unworthy of their love and care, lest they pull their hand away and we are left with nothing at all.

Family is the beginning and the end; you are the center who needs to hold on strong to both.

Family in the Bible

*"Honor your father and your mother, that your days may be long in the land that the Lord your God is giving you." – **Exodus 20:12***

It is not only our responsibility as Christians to be good to our mother, father, and all those who depend on us and on whom we depend, but it is also a way to please the Lord. The holy trinity includes the father, the Son, and Holy Spirit, thereby including the utmost importance of family in the very foundation of religion. The family gives us life, and we ought to be grateful to them for providing us with the chance to see a world so beautiful, created by a God so beautiful, and for experiences that are even more beautiful in themselves.

"Behold, children are a heritage from the Lord, the fruit of the womb a reward. Like arrows in the hand of a warrior are the children of one's youth. Blessed is the man who fills his quiver with them! He shall not be put to shame when he speaks with his enemies in the gate." – **Psalm 127:3-5**

When we are children, our parents fulfill our needs. When we are grown up, and our parents are old, we help them fulfill their needs. Child is the father of man, eventually. It is the cycle of life: we are all rendered helpless at some point in our lives. Providence has kept caretakers for us at all the stages in life in the form of family. Besides the essential love and support that we need to thrive, we find resources to live better and longer in the family.

Hold your family close and embrace them while you have the strength. It is one of the sweetest blessings of God and one that we also tend to take for granted. Do not make that mistake if you wish to be blissful and successful in all walks of life.

"Let love be genuine. Abhor what is evil; hold fast to what is good." – *Romans 12:9*

Thoughts to Ponder

- The only source of unconditional love in the world is God and your parents.

- Family is where you begin the lesson of gratitude, faith, and humor

- The Lord comforts us as a mother comforts her child.

- Family, where life begins, and Love never ends!

Chapter 5: Reach Out To Make a Difference

People give themselves different reasons for working towards success: some say they wish to make money to live a good life and provide their family with a good life. Some want to help those who cannot help themselves, and some do it purely to have some power over others. The motives are different for achieving 'success' for everyone. However, it might surprise some to know that the definition of success is also different as the personalities and traits of people vary from one another.

Success is Relative

The concept of success is relative. Some people associate it with having uncountable amounts of money, as they see money as the only source of bliss or happiness. According to them, it solves all the problems and makes life worth living. To others, success means a content family life. As long as they have a healthy and growing family that dines together and helps one another in times of need, they are successful. Some more concepts of success include giving back to the community: people who have grown in a community and seen prosperity wish to give back to it in terms of financial or temporal help, that is success for them; achieving a goal: being able to do something accurately and on time means success for some.

Whichever meaning one may believe in, the aim of every successful person should be to utilize their success, whether earned by hard work or passed on by someone above them, should be to reach out to others and make a difference in their lives. A successful life that benefits no one but the person himself, alone, would soon be found to be empty of substance and purpose.

Sharing is Earning

In your own way, make sure you help someone by sharing a little of your success or the means through which you achieved it with them. If it is a skill you have mastered and won numerous accolades for it, do not keep the knowledge to yourself; go out and spread it among those willing to learn it. If it is money you have earned, give charity to the destitute. If it is a happy family you have in your house, help your unhappy neighbor who might be suffering in his or her own house. Whatever it is that God has given you and makes you feel successful, share a little of it with those around you to show thanks to Him so that your success may retain and He may keep providing you with more.

"It is every man's obligation to put back into the world at least the equivalent of what he takes out of it." -Albert Einstein.

It is the science of things to balance both sides in order to make a working system. Harmony is the direct consequence of balance. Therefore, if you wish to be more successful in whatever you do, give more. Reach out to bigger populations to make a difference, and you will see the difference in your own fate, growing threefold and tenfold with time.

Suit Yourself

While you give back, there is no set way of doing it. Our varying personalities require unique methods of going about life. Our goals are our own, developed by our mind, which has been nurtured in an environment known only to us. The path to success is laden with many sets of hurdles and blocks for each of us, not guaranteeing everyone's same course of action. If we achieved success differently from the person standing next to us, then choosing to reach out to make a difference would also be according to our own personalities.

Take a deep breath before you set out to give back to the world. You need to know, first and foremost, how your goals are tied to who you are as a person. Your ideologies, your values, and your beliefs would need to stand aligned with your actions as you proceed. Setting your mind to something requires a thorough understanding of that task's dynamics and what it asks of the person performing it. For example, if you are a man of God and the charity you are expected to give might contribute to a Church's damage, then your heart will be conflicted. Likewise, in all matters of life, it is important to check to whom we are reaching out and how the help we give reflects on ourselves.

Never Stop

Persistence is key before and after success is achieved. To think that one can stop working after they have achieved a certain goal would be a folly. Hard work should never stop; the cost of standing out among others who are trying every day to reach glory is to mimic them in their efforts but outsmarting them in being persistent. Even when you have everything you once wanted, keep trying every day to maintain that success. To let go would mean being an audience to the gradual downfall of your empire.

We are what we repeatedly do. Excellence, then, is not an act but a habit. -Aristotle

Aristotle, the greatest among all philosophers, also recommends persistence as the answer to excellence, which would eventually become a habit as you go. Moreover, another advantage of persisting in your goals is that it enables you to leave a legacy for those behind you.

Always and Forever

Continuous hard work and effort help build strong foundations for your legacy. True success lasts even in the hereafter. Having achieved your goals for this world, you can work towards ensuring that the people you want to share it with keep reaping the fruits of the seeds you sowed.

Please think about your legacy because you are writing it every day. **- Gary Vaynerchuk**

Besides you, your neighbor, brother, sister, father, mother, and every person you know needs to try, if not succeed, to make a difference. There needs to be a collective effort on every man, woman, and child in this world to contribute to making this world a better place. By doing what we are obliged to and meeting our little aims, we would be doing the whole world a favor. Individual success rises to a collective level in no time.

Teach by example. Let those around you see your honesty, hard work, and the success that comes out of it as a happy consequence. Let them adopt the same ways, and see the world as it grows greener and brighter around you, one day at a time.

Thoughts to Ponder

- Changes begin at home
- You need to step on the first step of the ladder to reach the last one.
- Stay consistent in your virtues to make a difference.

Chapter 6: The Darker the Night, The Brighter the Light

"Always remember you are braver than you believe, stronger than you seem, smarter than you think, and twice as beautiful as you've ever imagined." -Dr. Seuss

We often tend to question ourselves when something goes wrong in our life. We ask ourselves if we deserved it, or was it a punishment for something we might have done wrong. While the answers may be different for each of us, it is a fact that we are all beautiful and strong. The only reason we suffer sometimes is that life, fate, and God wish to prepare for us better and brighter circumstances. The darker the night, the brighter the light.

If life was a garden where the flowers always bloomed and the Sun always shone, would we value the warmth anymore? If autumn never came and trees bore fruit all year, would we long for them? If happiness was constant, would we be able to enjoy it? The answer is no. The world is a system of differences and binaries where one thing derives its values from another. The night makes us look forward to sunrise, and only when it gets dark do we know for sure that there will be light.

Hardships often prepare ordinary people for an extraordinary destiny. **C.S. Lewis**

Challenging times in life are not only necessary, so we could value the easy and pleasant times but also so we could rise up stronger than we were when life went smoothly. To wish for an easy life is to wish for stagnancy. When an object is not moving, only then do flies and insects make a home on it. But if it is moving and growing, everyone around it is wary and alert, lest it might attack. Hence, the best kind of life one ought to wish for and strive towards is one that is challenging. Difficulties and adversities make us question our past states of mind and help us transform them into better versions of themselves.

When times are difficult, we find ourselves reacting to it in ways we never thought were possible. A herculean strength rises in us, enabling us to fend off the strongest winds and keep our boat sailing.

*"Challenges are what make life interesting, and overcoming them is what makes life meaningful." – **Joshua J. Marine***

The image of a heartbeat is made up of highs and lows; if the image is only a straight line with no crests and troughs, it means that the person is dead. Difficulty and ease are interconnected, and one cannot exist without the other. Weeds grow where there is greenery, and winds blow where there is scorching sunshine – you cannot have one without the other. One ought to cherish the challenges life throws at him because they are opportunities that will help him see things from a better perspective and prosper as a result.

Failure and Success

What feels like failure may just be a stepping stone towards success in the long term. As the saying goes, *"when one door closes, another opens."* If one thing goes wrong, it only is so because another is planning to go right for you. When God puts a man in difficulty, He tests him to see if he has enough patience to be worthy of the success He has been planning and keeping in store for him.

*"After every storm, the sun will smile; for every problem, there is a solution, and the soul's indefeasible duty is to be of good cheer." – **William R. Alger***

What a person can do then is to stay resolved and stringent in the face of hardships because they are a direct indication of better times. Success and failure, like day and night, are interconnected and bound to each other. Such is the world's reality, and such is the system of the God Almighty, full of paradoxes and amazing truths.

The Bible Says

Do not fear, for I have redeemed you; I have called you by name, you are mine. When you pass through the waters, I will be with you; and through the rivers, they shall not overwhelm you; when you walk through fire, you shall not be burned, and the flame shall not consume you, for I am the Lord you God, the Holy One of Israel, your Savior. **Isaiah 43:1-3**

The presence of God with us in bad times is proof that they are going to turn into good times. Wherever He is, evil cannot persist much longer. If you believe in His powers and omnipotence, then the concept of failure would be foreign to you completely. Even when others will be able to tell from the outside that you have fallen down, you will know that it only seems to because God is about to offer His helping hand.

Even if you walk through the proverbial fire of adversities, you will not be burned if God is by your side. Therefore, fear not when the night is dark. Stars shine bright when the sky is stark dark, and they hint towards the coming of the day.

I have told you all this so that you may have peace in me. Here on Earth, you will have many trials and sorrows. But take heart because I have overcome the world." **John 16:33**

Trials and sorrows are constant, but what can vary is our reaction to them. It is fully and wholly in our own hands how we decide to deal with matters and events that shake the ground from beneath our feet. We can fall down and stay there or get up and try again. If we choose to stay where we fell, we might never be able to get up. However, if we decide to rise above the tragedy that has struck us, we would be reaching the heights of glory sooner than later. We ought to take heart because God is watching over us and will surely guide us when we get lost. We are humans, and we are fallible, after all.

Thoughts to Ponder

- Absence makes the heart grow fonder

- "Let there be light," God said when there was only darkness

- You are a failure only if you think you are

- If we had no rain, we would lie in a desert.

Chapter 7: Success Is Unending, Failure Is Never Final

If you fail once, you learn a number of ways of getting up and about what not to do the next time. If you succeed, you know what it is like to have achieved the fruits of your work. And so, even if your supposed success is taken away, you still have the means to the end stored in your mind and heart, enabling you to retain the same success whenever and however you wish. Hence, *success is unending; failure is never final.*

Failure is a Teacher

God puts difficulties on our path in life on purpose: He loves to test those from whom He expects the most. He loves to see the extent to which His believer would bear and be patient to earn the reward of the test and His favor and grace. Furthermore, He knows that the strongest are those who keep moving forward in the face of downfalls because they know that God will lift them up when the time comes. Such people with strong wills and big hearts know all about faith, gratitude, and the importance of humor in life. Their hearts are embellished with the virtues of patience, the love of service, and truthfulness to the mission of God Almighty.

My flesh and my heart may fail,

but God is the strength of my heart

and my portion forever. **Psalm 73:26**

Failures are for a limited time in life; they stay only for so long as to teach a person how to navigate better through the road map to fulfill their goals. Failures are like stepping stones, some may be slippery, and some may have sharp edges, but in the end, they will take you to your destination, to the summit where you had always wanted to reach. A little discomfort and pain is the price we pay for glory and salvation. So if you fail, do not lose heart, for you are only *getting closer to your goal.*

"For I know the plans I have for you," declares the Lord, *"plans to prosper you and not to harm you, plans to give you hope and a future."* ***Jeremiah 29:11***

We can use failures to our advantage to make something beautiful from them; a lump of carbon under intense heat and pressure turns into a diamond. Just like we utilize scarps to make something of use—they are called DIY projects in today's age—we can carve and mend our moments of failure to renew them and transform them into something beautiful for ourselves and those around us.

If your business suffers losses, for example, and you fail financially, you can take the remaining resources that you cannot spend anywhere else to donate to the poor and the underprivileged. Sure, you failed for the world to see, but by feeding a few souls, you will have elevated your heart and soul. The world would have received something beautiful from the same failure it saw you suffer. Therefore, if you fail—because you will, we all do—do not take it to heart so as to disable it from seeing the possibilities that lie ahead. Instead, use it to create something pure and useful. Recycle failure into success!

Examples from Real Life

There are people around you in this world who suffered immense failure but decided not to let it get to them. They chose to keep pushing and stopping only when they had made a difference and achieved success out of their failure. One such example is Jack Ma, the founder of the Alibaba E-Commerce website. He was a man of little privilege who was born into a lower-middle-class family in China and started his career as an English teacher at $12 a month! He was rejected 30 times by the same place and was the only person among the 24 people who applied for jobs at KFC when it came to China who did not get selected. Moving on, two of his business ventures terribly failed, and he had nothing to go by for a long time. Today, he is the richest man in China and one of the richest in the world with an estimated net worth of $25 Billion, all because he did not let his failures overwhelm him, instead choosing to reshape them into success.

Steve Jobs, the late founder of Apple Inc., started off the now trillion-dollar enterprise with only two people in a garage. He was fired from his own company before he could reach the levels of success he is known for today.

Abraham Lincoln failed in business and presidential elections before becoming the great personality revered across all of America. Bill Gates is a Harvard drop-out, and Albert Einstein was expelled from his school multiple times. All of these people took their apparent failures and turned them into incredible successes for the world to marvel at. They now enjoy the fruits of their hard work generated directly from the force of their failures.

Give Yourself the Grounds

If you wish to succeed, it is essential that you must allow yourself to fail first. If you give a child a bicycle to ride and tell him he will learn it without falling, you would be lying to him. The child will lose balance and fall many times before he will learn how to ride it well. Those falls will be the lessons for him in what to do and what not to do. He will have tasted failure, seen it up close enough to work his way towards a steady and safe ride. If he never fell, he would not know the importance of riding with a stable posture.

Give yourselves the grounds to fail, and you will soon be enjoying the fruits of never-ending success. Experiment, try, and practice multiple times before you settle on a method of doing anything.

I've not failed; I've just found 10,000 ways that won't work! **Thomas Edison**

The destination that is reached through the most complex of routes looks the sweetest. We cherish the success received after long periods of effort. A farmer waits all year to harvest his crop; in the meantime, he sees draughts and storms but does not give up on his job. It is our job as humans and the subjects of God overseeing us not to give up when we fall. To get up, continue and create glory out of failure is the way to go in life!

Thoughts to Ponder

- Stars shine brighter when the night is dark

- We only reap what we sow, nothing more and nothing less

- Mountains would not go uphill if success was supposed to be a linear path

Chapter 8: Proper Prior Planning Prevents Poor Performance

The 6P fact stands true in all aspects of life: **Proper Prior Planning Prevents Poor Performance**. Besides adopting a thorough attitude of gratitude, faith, and humor in our lives, we need to learn empirical methods of going about everyday life smoothly and steadily.

The key to success, however, you may define it, is to know beforehand what you wish to achieve and have a plan for it. Doing your homework and learning all there is to learn about the task you want to perform is not only wise but helpful in the long run. It makes moving from one task to another easier, as the process gets streamlined and quickened.

Craft a Plan

Before you step into the maze, it is essential you look at its map and assess it for possible routes that will lead you to your destination. While it is adventurous to find your way through living it, it can be quite frustrating and painstaking to get lost more than once. True, failure does teach us many important lessons in life, but to be fooled twice or even thrice is a sign of you not taking the correct measures. Sometimes, looking out for yourself and consulting a map beforehand is the best course of action, instead of letting the incessant struggle consume all your time and energy.

If you wish to climb a mountain, for example, you would be putting your life in danger if you do not refer to guides and references that would explain the process to you. Intelligence is understanding something, genius is perfecting a skill, but wisdom is knowing the difference between the two. It is having confidence in your limits so as to enable yourself to surpass them by taking help where it is needed.

Crafting a plan for anything and everything in life is critical – its benefits countless and its outcomes incomparable. Take the example of starting a business: numerous plans go into effect for a venture to kick start and make its way to the top. Initial financial and time investment, hiring resources and approaching sponsors, setting up finances, building an HR, finding an appropriate location, and devising efficient marketing strategies. All of these steps are planned before the business is even inaugurated to ensure stability and profits and avoid any risks of loss. When we put big things in life at stake, such as our life's worth of money or our own lives, as in the case of climbing mountains, it is crucial to have a plan –access to the road map for the journey we are setting out to cover.

Even when matters are not as grand as climbing a mountain or starting a business, it never hurts to be more organized. It helps us and nobody else, but not staying organized harms us *and* those depending upon us. Therefore, it is better to make a list, write it down, get it tallied, have it surveyed, and repeat it all twice, just so you can achieve your long-set goal with ease, timeliness, and comfort.

Ways of Planning

Let's say you plan to visit a library on the weekend to gather reading material on a subject on which you wish to do research and learn more about. Can you simply go there and, standing in front of tall shelves, expect it all to magically make sense to you? Of course not! In order to know where to begin, what to do, and how to proceed, you need to be sure of your course of action. You need to know the genre of books you are looking for: researches, fiction, biographies, or memoirs; which will it be? You need to know how many books you need in total: six, eight, ten, how many? Other considerations will include: How many days does the library rent? For how long can you keep them? Do you even have a membership?

All these things need to be known before the process starts. This is called **Research**. If you are buying a car, as another instance, the features of all the models within your price range should be in your knowledge if you are to make a smart and calculated decision. Research is the most vital step for the execution and attainment of anything in life. A way you can manage your findings of said research is through **Journaling**.

It can be challenging to keep track of all the methods and techniques found and learned over the process of research. The human mind can only retain so much in memory; it is only normal for one to forget one or two things in a process complex enough. To avoid missing any bit of information that may set the basis for future action, you can write it all down in a journal in the form of rough sheets, bullet points, or notes to help you when you need them. It is not a childish thing to do; accepting that you can forget facts and names is okay as none of us are superhumans with photographic memories.

By using research and journaling to help yourself, you will be speeding up the process of achieving your goal and reaching high levels of accuracy. The most mindful and successful people in the world work this way. They plan ahead and make a map because they believe in the 6P fact: Proper Prior Planning Prevents Poor Performance. Life does not give all of us the chance to rise up from the quicksand of poor performance once we fall deep into it.

The Bible Says

It is a quality of the Almighty Himself to plan and then act. He has made us in His image, and so it is only fair that we also stay prepared for that which comes ahead. While in Judah, our Lord Jesus Christ made an incredible plan for a man named Boaz to marry Ruth. The demise of Ruth's husband had made her poor, and so He provided for her and gave them a child, Naomi, by planning to give her Boaz as a husband. The Bible says of their coming together:

Diligence promises well, both for this world and the other. **Ruth 2:1-3 (Matthew Henry Commentary)**

Furthermore, in the book of Genesis, we see that God promised Abraham the Land of Canaan, numerous offspring, and 'blessings unto the world.' These promises were God's symbols of knowledge and control over the world. And while we as mortal humans may never match that kind of greatness in planning, we can humbly strive to reach the lowest levels of it by applying this strategy in our lowly lives.

What is a quality of the merciful God can never bring His creation, man, down. It is bound to make him rise above himself and help him achieve the best of the best. Thus, make a plan and stick to it if you wish to reach the heights of glory.

Thoughts to Ponder

- You can say more only when you know what has already been said
- The policies of national and international governments come into being after years of planning
- Research is the first step to action

Chapter 9: Life Gets Easier If You Plow Around The Stumps!

When it comes to certain tasks, completing them looks no different than making an elephant pass through the needle hole. However, in reality, when we set our mind to it and get working, it feels as easy as slicing a piece of cake. Appearances can be scary; besides just being deceiving, they can make us believe that we are incapable of performing a task and will be grossly affected by said inabilities. When, in fact, that is not the case. We are very much capable of ticking off one box after another on our to-do list if we stick to a few simple methods:

1) **Use your plus-points:** All of us are unique in our good and bad qualities. While we should try to improve the bad ones, there is no shame in leveraging the good ones for your benefit and in pursuit of your goals. If, say, you have leadership capabilities that enable you to manage things well, instead of suppressing them so as to not come off as 'strict,' apply them to make your tasks easier for yourself. Use your plus-points!

2) **Do your homework:** As explained in the previous chapter, *Proper Prior Planning Prevents Poor Performance*. So before you sit down to carry out a task, make sure you know all about what you are doing.

3) **Control your emotions:** By that, I don't mean you to become a robot by suppressing all your emotions. What is meant by 'control' here is being moderate. Often, in work environments, we tend to get frustrated, and anger gets the best of us. It is necessary that we keep our emotions in check while working towards a goal so as not to hinder our progress in any way.

4) **Use your willpower:** In the face of apparent failure, do not lose faith. No matter how bad things are going, if you believe that you can turn them around, you surely will. The making and breaking of your timeline

to reach a goal depend entirely upon your willpower. The determination and belief towards something positively affect our physical response to it.

5) Stay focused: Distractions can increase the distance between you and your goals. Make sure your sight is set on that one thing you wish to get close to, and that thing only. Any and all objects in between and around should not catch your attention. If you are to achieve a goal successfully and on time, stay focused!

To Each Their Own

People are born different, each a unique experiment onto themselves. It is futile to want to be like someone else, someone famous and more successful than you. Their path was different, and yours varies from theirs. The things they have achieved in their life do not compare with your struggle. If it did, they would be the same person as you. The fact that God made many of us with many different qualities should tell you that He intends for you to make your own ways towards your goals.

It is best to recognize your own qualities as standing apart from your companions and friends and then try to reach your destination in life. Dr. Seuss said:

"Today you are You, that is truer than true. There is no one alive who is Youer than You."

Make your own shovel, dig your own well and carry your own water. People will come and go, lend you a hand, and ignore you at times, but you will have yourself available to yourself in all times and circumstances. So value your own presence, embrace your attributes gifted by God and make use of them to get what you want in life.

Plow around the Stumps

Before planting crops on a piece of land, farmers have to first clear the land. Before the advent of the advanced machinery of today, farmers carried out this task with their hands. While doing so, they often faced stumps that made clearing difficult. So, instead of wasting all their time and energy on the difficult, even impossible stumps, they would simply move on to plow around the stumps, over the land that did allow them to do it smoothly.

And, just like these farmers of yore, it is wise for us not to waste our time and energy on things that cannot be solved or resolved. The desire to have all things calculated and decided is inherent in all humans, and while it is advantageous in most settings, it can be harmful and digressive in some. Not all stumps can be cleared and broken; they are stubborn and require a tremendous commitment in energy and attention. It is wise not to spend all we have on the stumps, the unbreakable disturbances in our lives. Instead, we ought to plow around them, work on the things that *can* be solved with an average or even minimum amount of time and energy.

It does not mean that we are lazy; it only means that we have our priorities straight and know what we are doing. To wish to be able to do everything is unhealthy. Life is not designed for us to be able to do it all. Some things have to be left as they are; we cannot resolve them if they do not wish to be resolved themselves. It is then only the will of God that can undo them and clear the metaphorical stump for the metaphorical honest farmer.

All of us deal with stumps on a daily basis: a boss who does not see eye to eye with us, a parent who cannot align their ideology with ours, or a friend who refuses to hold on to the promises they made. We can try our best to work *on* them and undo them to the best of our capabilities, but when it does not work and all else fails, it is okay to work *around* them.

So do not fret too much over things that are out of your control, and pay attention to those that can be helped. Life is too short to be spent on the impossible aspects of it. Use your own road map, be your own navigator, decide which streets you ought to turn to reach the final destination towards which you have been driving since day one. Remember: if there are stumps in your way that refuse to move, go around them!

Thoughts to Ponder:

- A fly sits someplace else if we shoo it away

- In their honest purity, children do not take 'no' for an answer

- Dealing with the easy things first gives you more time for the difficult

Chapter 10: Faith Will See You Through

"Therefore, since we have been made right in God's sight by faith, we have peace with God because of what Jesus Christ our Lord has done for us. Because of our faith, Christ has brought us into this place of undeserved privilege where we now stand, and we confidently and joyfully look forward to sharing God's glory." **(Romans 5:1-2)**

At least once in our lives, we all have pondered over the abstract of faith. We all know what having faith means, though it is challenging for some of us to have faith in things we cannot perceive. Most of us believe in God, but only a few of us have faith in Him. Hence they are oblivious to the fact that faith is a magical power.

Not many people know this, but there is an absolute correlation between faith and power in the Bible, and when we make the right choices in life, God rewards us with more power and strength to strive in life. That is how we meet success. How faith helps us in life and gives us power may still be a mystery to most of us, but not something we cannot learn.

"He did not do many mighty works there because of their unbelief." **(Matthew 13:58)**

The above sermon talks about the essentiality of having faith. The more faith we have in God, the more we allow him into our lives, rewarding us with more power and strength. According to the Bible, Abraham was the father of faith, and God's commentary on his life is a prime example of the power we are blessed with when we have faith.

"Now faith is the full assurance of things hoped for, the evidence of things not seen." **(Hebrews 11:1)**

Importance of Faith in Becoming Successful

Now, we've discussed that having faith grants us ultimate power and strength that can help us overcome any challenge in life and success. If we have complete faith in God, then here are some things that will help us excel in life:

We Stop Worrying

We worry about the future when we only trust as far as we understand. In everyone's life, there are various hardships and trials. Most of us are more likely to mull over these challenges until we die because nobody but God knows the purpose behind these hardships and trials. Similarly, when we talk about the future, there is a whole lifetime of unforeseen circumstances.

However, if we choose to trust God with these problems, we are freed from worrying about life. When we have faith in Him, we also develop a sense of understanding that whatever will happen will happen for good because now, we have given the planner of planners the steering wheel of our lives.

"Casting all your care upon Him, for He cares for you." **(Peter 5:7)**

We Become Confident and Strong

Have you ever tried to do something you're passionate about but failed? Often, we come up against our shortcomings when we try to do good in life. Our problem is that we become too aware of all the things we lack and tend to say mean things to our loved ones, especially those who are weaker than us. When we don't have faith in God, we are more likely to welcome dismay over our own incapabilities while we are facing these shortcomings.

"For the eyes of the Lord run to and fro throughout the whole earth, to show Himself strong on behalf of those whose heart is loyal to Him." **(2 Chronicles 16:9)**

However, when we have faith in the Almighty, there is a guarantee of not muddling along in our strength.

"And the God of peace will crush Satan under your feet shortly." **(Roman 16:20)**

If we have faith in God and believe in the scriptures and the mentioned verses, indeed, God will crush Satan under our feet, restoring our confidence that ultimately will boost our confidence and help us succeed in life.

We Become Invincible

In Matthew 7:24-27, we can learn about the essentiality of why faith should be the foundation of every human. Jesus tells us that whoever hears His sayings and does them will be like a man who builds his house on a rock. No matter what storm comes and beats against it, it will remain standing. On the other hand, people who trust worldly things are like a man who builds his house on sand.

So by believing in God and opting to live with fate makes us stronger against the treacherous waters that every human must learn to swim through in order to find success.

We Experience Joy

"Being confident of this very thing, that He who has begun a good work in you will complete it until the day of Jesus Christ." **(Philippians 1:6)**

When we develop faith in God, He begins to work in us to set us free from our sinful nature, transforming us into His image. When we are cleansed, we are then bestowed with a feeling of joy and positivity in life. With that positivity, we can easily accomplish our goals and become successful in life.

In the end, there was a period throughout the entire existence of every great thing and every great person when they were not great. However, despite that, they succeeded. That by itself is proof that more is conceivable than we might be capable of right now. We should have faith in what in the far future is predestined for us. We ought to have faith far beyond what we can see today.

Seeing the limitations of science and making the conscious effort to suspend reason and accept the truth on faith is essential. It is what helps us believe in powers greater than ourselves. Faith is *"being sure of what we hope for and certain of what we do not see."* (Hebrews 11:1)

We have faith in science. We believe that truth can be found through perception, estimation, and analysis and in the formulation, testing, and alteration of speculations. We should likewise accept that there are real factors that fall outside of these limits. Furthermore, to trust in them with life and guts requires faith in the unseen. So, if your wife is mowing the lawn, don't ask her when the supper is going to be ready. Instead, have faith that God will not let you sleep with an empty belly.

Thoughts to Ponder

- God would not have put a dream in your heart if He did not equip you with what you need to make that dream a reality.

- *"Many are the plans in a man's heart, But it is the Lord's purpose that Prevails"* **Proverbs 19:21**

- Good, Better, Best, You never let it rest Until the good is better and the better is best.

- Some people don't plan to fail. They just fail to plan.

- Most people will say the most washed in 2020 were the hands. I will disagree and say it was the brain.

Chapter 11: The Joy of Living Is The Joy Of Giving

"Life is not always easy to live, but the opportunity to do so is a blessing beyond comprehension. In the process of living, we will face struggles, many of which will cause us to suffer and to experience pain." **L. Lionel Kendrick**

Once in our life, we all have pondered over the question of whether life is a blessing or a curse. We have made an abode in a world where we constantly struggle with relationships, financial and health crises, career pressure, boredom, emptiness, etc. Eventually, we develop a sense that life is instead a curse than a blessing because we fail to realize all the blessings that we have bestowed upon us. Hence, we become oblivious to the joys of life.

We must always believe that there has to be a starting point of how we all started because life is too complex to have happened on its own. For example, the birth itself is a miracle because watching a child grow is one of the most beautiful things in this world.

Suppose we look into the anatomy of human beings. In that case, we will conclude that this is one of the most extraordinary things. Its miraculous structure and function could never evolve automatically without a wise designer behind it. Hence, God is the creator behind this mystery of life that we live routinely, and if we learn to trust him, we will find joy in life.

"Blessed are they who see beautiful things in humble places where other people see nothing." **Camille Pissarro**

Once upon a time, there was a young girl whose brother passed away. Following his death, she came to the point in her life where her faith in God started to fade away. She felt helpless because even after all the praying she had done, God refused to bring her brother back to her. The scar etched onto her heart was profound; she knew it could not heal or fade. After all the troubles that came into her life, her parents never lost faith in God. She observed her parents, and eventually, she regretted blaming God for taking her brother's life. In spite of the fact that He just blessed her with eleven years to spend time with her brother, she thanked him. She realized those eleven years were a blessing in her life. With that, she learned that if God wanted, He could not have blessed her with those eleven years of happiness and unforgettable memories, but He did.

In the end, she established a firm belief that life is a blessing from God no matter how long because he gave her the opportunity to live her life, and so we have to appreciate every minute that we have in this world. Each of us is only here for a time, and none of us can assume that we'll be here tomorrow because, indeed, life is uncertain.

To see the beauty that adorns the world and our lives, we must become familiar with our surroundings with an open mind. As humans, we tend to the bad surrounding us and ignore all the good things, hand in hand, taking place in our lives; and that is how we fail to find the joy in life.

Part II

A Chinese saying states, "If you want happiness for an hour, take a nap. If you want happiness for a day, go fishing. If you want happiness for a year, inherit a fortune. If you want happiness for a lifetime, help somebody." Therefore, as great thinkers have suggested over the centuries, joy is found in helping others.

It is beautiful to offer than to receive. The admired apothegm is embedded into our heads from a very young age. However, is there a more profound truth behind the adage?

The resonating answer is yes. Scientific research gives convincing information to help the narrative evidence that giving is an excellent pathway to self-awareness and lasting satisfaction. Through MRI technology, we currently realize that giving enacts the very parts of the brain that are stimulated by food and sex. Experiments show evidence that selflessness is designed in mind—and it is pleasurable. Helping other people may simply be the key to carrying on with a daily existence that is not just more joyful yet additionally better, more well off, more beneficial, and significant.

The power of giving is showed in the graciousness and liberality that we offer to another person. At the point when we give another unselfishly, the vibrational energy radiating from our inner mind is at its most potent. The force of offering, as indicated by neuroscience, is that it feels better.

If we find ourselves feeling miserable and unhappy, we must make someone happy and see what happens. If we feel drained and unfulfilled, then we should take a stab at doing some meaningful and worthwhile work and see how we feel. The catch is that we should accomplish this work with enthusiasm and passion.

Numerous institutions, organizations, and people are occupied with exemplary works of giving. Narayanan Krishnan is a graduate move on from Madurai, India, who gave up on his profession as a chef with a five-star hotel when he saw a man so ravenous that he was feeding on his own excreta. From that point on, Krishnan began his honorable initiative to take care of thousands of destitute and vagrants in his state—free from cost.

I encourage you to search for promising opportunities where you can give and help other people. The endowment of happiness will come to you when you give of yourself to other people. That is what is the issue here. We should rehearse and submit our lives to giving delight. Try it! It works!

"And God is able to bless you abundantly so that in all things at all times, having all that you need, you will abound in every good work." **2 Corinthians 9:8**

On the other hand and in the end, we should all look to the Lord to give us the strength to overcome disappointments by knowing He is still in control, giving us the faith to stay:

- **Calm**

He says, "Be still, and know that I am God. I will be exalted among the nations, I will be exalted in the earth." **(Psalm 46:10)**

- **Compassionate**

"Be kind to one another, tenderhearted, forgiving one another, as God in Christ forgave you." **(Ephesians 4:32)**

- **Constructive**

"All things are lawful," but not all things are helpful. "All things are lawful," but not all things build up." **(1 Corinthians 10:23)**

- **Challenged**

"But if anyone does not provide for his relatives, and especially for members of his household, he has denied the faith and is worse than an unbeliever." **(1 Timothy 5:8)**

- **Connected**

Long ago, at many times and in many ways, God spoke to our fathers by the prophets, but in these last days, he has spoken to us by his Son, whom he appointed the heir of all things, through whom also he created the world. He is the radiance of the glory of God and the exact imprint of his nature, and he upholds the universe by the word of his power. After making purification for sins, he sat down at the right hand of the Majesty on high, having become as much superior to angels as the name he has inherited is more excellent than theirs. For to which of the angels did God ever say, "You are my Son, today I have begotten you"? Or again, "I will be to him a father, and he shall be to me a son"? *(Hebrews 1:1-14)*

- **Confident.**

"Though an army encamp against me, my heart shall not fear; though war arise against me, yet I will be confident." (Psalm 27:3)

- **Centered.**

"Do not repay evil for evil or reviling for reviling, but on the contrary, bless, for to this you were called, that you may obtain a blessing." (1 Peter 3:9)

- **Consistent.**

"And if you faithfully obey the voice of the Lord your God, being careful to do all his commandments that I command you today, the Lord your God will set you high above all the nations of the earth. And all these blessings shall come upon you and overtake you if you obey the voice of the Lord your God. Blessed shall you be in the city, and blessed shall you be in the field. Blessed shall be the fruit of your womb and the fruit of your ground and the fruit of your cattle, the increase of your herds and the young of your flock. Blessed shall be your basket and your kneading bowl." (Deuteronomy 28:1-68)

- **Committed.**

*"Therefore a man shall leave his father and his mother and hold fast to his wife, and they shall become one flesh." **(Genesis 2:24)***

- **Convinced.**

*"For I am sure that neither death nor life, nor angels nor rulers, nor things present nor things to come, nor powers, nor height nor depth, nor anything else in all creation, will be able to separate us from the love of God in Christ Jesus our Lord." **(Romans 8:38-39)***

Thoughts to Ponder:

- You will keep in perfect peace those whose minds are steadfast because they trust in you. *(Isaiah 26:3)*

Chapter 12: What Is The Legacy You Want?

"If you would not be forgotten as soon as you are dead, either write something worth reading or do something worth writing." **-Benjamin Franklin**

The legacy we leave is essential for progressing the foundations of life. We live in a world left by the people who preceded us. And the people who will come after us will have just what we leave them. We are stewards of this world, and we have a calling to leave it better than how we thought it was, regardless of whether it seems like a small contribution.

Legacies have crude force for good and evil. Some people have changed the world for good, people who have opened up new worlds for a large number of others, people who have prodded others onto new statures. Moreover, some people have caused enormous destruction for incalculable millions, who left a wake of torment. What we do influences others. Our lives can make good or furnish evil. So, we must do good.

So, how do you want people to remember you when you're no more? What story is your life composing that will be left for a long time into the future? These are profound questions to consider about what sort of legacy your life will leave. Here are different ways of leaving a legacy.

Live your inheritance

Our kids hear us out most eagerly by watching us live. So live with character, conviction, and enthusiasm. The most permanent legacy is the way we choose to live.

Live as you mean it

Draw in this life with gratitude and passion. None of us realize how long our lives might be. Yet, we can leave the legacy of living as we give it a second thought and live in such a way that praises our creation. People will recollect how you live more than the details of your accomplishments.

Love unconditionally

"Loving our spouse and our children with commitment and enthusiasm is a legacy like no other." **Anonymous**

In any event, when we don't have anything else to give, we actually have love. Loving our children and spouse is a legacy like no other.

Keep Writing

Build up the propensity for keeping a normal record of what's significant in your life. One All Pro Dad we know just kept notes in the front of his Bible. Scribble down key occasions like births, weddings, and accomplishments alongside a remark or two. At the point when he died, it ended up being beyond value.

Share stories of the past with your family.

Be very easy to read and share your stories with your children. Kids lean toward these even to Harry Potter; telling them about your life can turn into a discussion they value well into adulthood.

Sharing your vision after you are departed.

Tell your kids what kids of life you expect them to live after you part ways from the human world. Having those thoughts continuously play through your kids' heads can help explore them as they face critical decisions. "How might Dad respond?" is the most remarkable legacy of all.

In action, we are constantly inspiring other people. However, it depends on us if we inspire them in a good way or a bad way. Our body language speaks for itself, and people notice that, especially children.

They learn from their elders and keep getting inspired by our actions and words. Hence, we must always do and speak well in front of others because we do not know whom we inspire.

Has anybody at any point propelled you to change yourself in a significant manner that made you better, more joyful, or more satisfied? Assuming this is the case, you comprehend the distinction that positive inspirations can make in a person's life. Inspiration is powerful, yet it is not easy to influence others into becoming the best version of themselves. Hence, this is why it is essential to leave a legacy behind because you can inspire people from it.

A great deal of us has a variety of "selves" that come out depending upon the social circumstance: home, work, and companions all require an alternate routine. Yet, putting on an alternate act for each gathering of individuals you experience is too debilitating, and it's surely not a decent method to inspire individuals around you. Would you put your trust in a person who was so awkward as a part of their character that they wanted to pander to whatever crowd they were with? Embrace your actual self without a statement of regret because that is how you leave your mark in this world.

Exploring alternative thoughts and ideas is another way of inspiring people around you. Any person who thinks they have every one of the appropriate answers is messing with themselves, so try testing your convictions consistently. In case you're monetarily conservative, investigate a thoroughly examined piece by somebody on the far edge of the political range so you can see the opposite side of the story. In case you're a Christian, investigate the contemplations of the most profoundly respected Muslims to find why they accept what they do. Have discussions with people who take uniquely in contrast to you do to realize what matters to them. It's impossible you'll adjust your perspective, and on the off chance that you genuinely accept something with conviction, it should hold up to examination. Your receptiveness will show others that you are so firm in your feelings that you're willing to challenge your beliefs. You'll additionally create trust in individuals who think uniquely in contrast to you do, who, in any case, may have been reluctant to move toward you.

And in the end, you must set people free. Don't simply offer people bit by bit guidance. Instead, allow them to sort it out themselves. Nobody prefers to be micromanaged. If you're requested to help, convey a harsh rule to get a person going the correct way. However, purposefully leave something left to the creative mind so they will have the opportunity to fill in the spaces. When a person finds they are fit for sorting things out by themselves, they will find they are more remarkable than they at any point expected.

When you inspire people into becoming the best version of themselves, they remember you for the legacy you left for them. And they convey that legacy to their children and juniors. Hence, making the world a better place.

Thoughts to Ponder

- "In the long run, a person who goes the second mile will be further ahead." *- Ed Roth*

- "Your life does not get better by chance it gets better by change."

- "Not everything that can be counted counts, and not everything that counts can be counted." *-Albert Einstein*

- "You make a living by what you get, but you make a life by what you give!" *-Winston Churchill*

- "The man or women who walk with God always get to their destination."

- "It's not what you gather, but what you scatter that tells what kind of life you have lived."

Chapter 13: Living Thoughtfully, Dying Well

"If we all did the things we are capable of, we would astound ourselves." **– Thomas Edison.**

Keeping a balance in life is essential, albeit a lot of people don't realize this. From a young age, by our parents or our teachers, a notion is embedded in our minds, i.e., life is about building a career and meeting needs. Although it is true, people sometimes get lost and forget to enjoy life. When they are old, these people live with regret for not living their life to the fullest. When it comes to enjoying life, it is crucial for us to have a clear mind before we commence on this journey, and to have a clear sense, we must look into Jesus's life.

When Jesus first called his disciples, they dropped everything to follow him:

"Passing alongside the Sea of Galilee, [Jesus] saw Simon and Andrew the brother of Simon casting a net into the sea, for they were fishermen. And Jesus said to them, 'Follow me, and I will make you become fishers of men.' And immediately, they left their nets and followed him. And going on a little farther, he saw James the son of Zebedee and John, his brother, who were in their boat mending the nets. And immediately he called them, and they left their father Zebedee in the boat with the hired servants and followed him" (Mark 1:16-20).

Jesus' earliest followers, in a real sense, dropped their jobs to follow him—they committed themselves to him. Similarly, we are called to do penances for Jesus—to show others love by giving, investing resources, and praying. For Jesus, conviction and actions are very much the same—you can't have one without the other. We should give whatever Jesus requests from us.

We must think about how we use our money. To a young rich man, Jesus says: "If you would be perfect, go, sell what you possess and give to the poor, and you will have treasure in heaven; and come, follow me" (Matthew 19:21; see 19:16-30).

With regards to our time and resources, Jesus has an altogether unique economy as a main priority. Is money standing between you and Jesus? How can you use it to help and empower the impoverished?

Regarding a poor widow who put a seemingly insignificant amount of money into the offering box, Jesus says: "Truly, I say to you, this poor widow has put in more than all those who are contributing to the offering box. For they all contributed out of their abundance, but she out of her poverty has put in everything she had, all she had to live on" (Mark 12:43-44; see Mark 12:41-44).

The cash of Jesus' realm is unique in relation to our own. Jesus' money is benevolence and love.

To a man with a recently lost love one, Jesus said: "'follow me.' But [the man] said [to Jesus], 'Lord, let me first go and bury my father.' And Jesus said to him, 'Leave the dead to bury their own dead. But as for you, go and proclaim the kingdom of God'" (Luke 9:59-60).

Jesus was not too far off, calling him face to face. Furthermore, this implied the man needed to act now. We as a whole have these minutes throughout everyday life: When Jesus advises us to act now, and we need to view him seriously when he says as much.

For Jesus, it's all about God's kingdom. For us, it too should be all about God's kingdom. From a different man, Jesus hears: "'I will follow you, Lord, but let me first say farewell to those at my home.' Jesus said to him, 'No one who puts his hand to the plow and looks back is fit for the kingdom of God'" (Luke 9:61-62).

There is no dithering in support of God's kingdom, and there is no thinking back—it's about the thing God is doing at this very moment. It's tied in with putting our hand to the furrow of God's work. On the off chance that you love God, you love the kingdom, and you love individuals. If you love the kingdom, you're not going to ask yourself what else is significant: you will live for the kingdom.

At the end of it all, Jesus notes that he will recognize those who follow him by whether or not they are caring for the impoverished, outsider, and marginalized. This is what the "least of these" passage is about (Matthew 25:31-46).

Jesus has also given us the mandate to bring the gospel to those who are yet to hear his name. Jesus' economy is not just about alleviating physical poverty; it's also about alleviating spiritual poverty. Jesus tells us to "make disciples of all nations" (Matthew 28:19-20).

God has requested that we exhibit our conviction by carrying the good news to the individuals who feel miserable. We are called to drop everything for him. This is what the issue here is: imagining what the world could resemble and joining God during the time spent making that vision a reality.

Jesus has called us to go along with him in his work—to put stock in it with all we have. The expense might be difficult to bear or comprehend on occasion. However, when it's placed in the viewpoint of all that Christ has accomplished for us—passing on for our transgressions—it seems like practically nothing. And in the end, if we live like this, we will live a happy life and won't have any regrets when we get old. Knowing we lived a life demonstrated by Jesus will also help us overcome the dread of dying. [1]

---

[1] 5 Ways to Really Live (and Give) Like Jesus. Retrieved from https://www.crosswalk.com/church/giving/5-ways-to-live-and-give-like-jesus.html

Thoughts to Ponder

- Faith and fear each demand that we believe in something we cannot see. The choice is ours.

- God's friendship prevails when human friendships fail.

- "Hold everything in your hands lightly. Otherwise, it hurts when God pries your fingers open." *- Corrie Ten Boom*

- It took the manager to bring God to man. But it took the cross to bring man to God.

- Family is the greatest legacy a person can have.

- Remember the "Boomer-rang" effect; whatever you do will always come back.

Chapter 14: Spirituality

What are spiritual needs?

Spirituality means different things to different people. Religion and faith might be part of someone's spirituality, but spirituality isn't always religious. Everyone has spiritual needs throughout their lives, whether they follow a religion or not. Spiritual needs can include:

- The need for meaning and purpose in our lives

- The need to love and feel loved

- The need to feel a sense of belonging

- The need to feel hope, peace, and gratitude.

People do different things to meet these spiritual needs, depending on what's important to them. Some people do things within their religion, such as prayer or going to a religious meeting. For other people, it could be being with friends and family, spending time in nature, or doing work or hobbies.

What's most important to someone can change over their lifetime.

Spiritual needs in terminal illness

Being diagnosed with a terminal illness often causes people to think about death, loss, and grief in ways they haven't had before.

Some people with a terminal illness may want to reflect on the meaning of their life, perhaps more so than at any other time in their life. Spiritual practice, including religion, may become more important to someone as they approach the end of their life.

Spiritual needs are connected to physical, emotional, and social needs too. Some studies have suggested that spiritual wellbeing may affect suffering at the end of life. Spiritual assessment and care are therefore critical when caring for someone with a terminal illness.

What is spiritual distress?

Spiritual wellbeing is often described as feeling at peace.

Spiritual distress – also called spiritual pain or suffering – can occur when people cannot find sources of meaning, hope, love, peace, comfort, strength, and connection in their life. This distress can also affect their physical and mental health. Terminal illness can often cause spiritual pain in patients as well as their family and friends.

How can I assess someone's spiritual needs?

Encourage patients to talk about how they're feeling. Someone might have unmet spiritual needs if they are:

. Searching for meaning, for example, asking questions such as 'Why is this happening?', 'Why me?', 'Who am I?' and 'How will I be remembered?'

- Becoming more withdrawn and isolated

- Afraid of being alone

- Refusing care

- Saying they feel scared or worried.

Many health and social care professionals find it hard to discuss spirituality with their patients. Some of the reasons for this include:

- Lack of training

- Not knowing what to say

- Being concerned about saying something inappropriate.

There are assessment tools you can use to start the conversation. One of these is the HOPE tool which is based on the questions below:

- What are your sources of hope, strength, comfort, and peace?

- Organized religion

- Do you have a religion or faith?

- How important is your faith, religion, or faith to you?

- Personal spirituality and practices

- What do you do that gives you a sense of meaning and purpose in life

- In what ways does this add to your sense of identity?

- Effects on medical care and of life issues

- Has being unwell stopped you from doing things that give your life meaning and purpose?

- Are there any specific practices we should know about in providing for your care?

If you feel unsure about what spirituality means or find it difficult to talk about it, you might find it helpful to assess yourself. It can help you to identify and explore your thoughts on spirituality.

How can I provide spiritual care?

All health and social care professionals can provide spiritual care, but some patients will want extra support from specialists such as chaplains or faith leaders.

Everyone's needs are different. Ask your patient what's important to them and what you can do to help.

Some people might have all their spiritual needs met by carrying out their practice. Others might need some practical help to do the essential things as their illness advances. For example, you might be able to help by arranging for them to attend a religious service, see a faith leader at home or where they are staying, be with family and friends, or spend time in nature.

Some people will need more support and may want to talk to you about their spiritual concerns. Encourage the person to explore their worries and fears. Listen without passing judgment or dismissing their concerns. Try to understand and listen to your patient's beliefs without imposing your own. If you don't feel comfortable having these conversations, ask an experienced colleague or a specialist such as a chaplain to be involved.

Questions about life and its meaning are very complex, so don't feel you always need to have an answer. Leave room for listening, thoughtfulness and stillness.

You can also encourage the patient to find their coping techniques, especially ones that have worked for them in the past. This may include doing things they enjoy, writing down thoughts and feelings, and finding ways to relax, such as listening to music or having a massage.

Some people may find it helpful to find out more about how they are feeling for themselves. You could suggest the patient reads our information on emotional and spiritual pain.

What is other support available?

Ask the person if they would like any other support. They may want to speak to a faith leader if they have a religion.

The local hospital, hospice, or palliative care team may have a chaplaincy service. Chaplains are trained specialists who work with all people of any or no religion to help them find meaning and explore what's important to them.

Talking to a psychologist or counselor, a specialist palliative care social worker, or going to a local support group may also be helpful.

Taking care of yourself

Caring for people with a terminal illness can be very demanding. It might prompt you to ask questions about your own mortality, your beliefs and look for meaning and purpose in your life. Take time to look after your own spiritual wellbeing. Spiritual self-care can involve spending time with family and friends, meditation, physical activity, reading, spending time in nature, and following religious practices. If you're struggling, you might find it helpful to speak to your manager, a counselor, a psychologist, or a faith leader.[2]

And with the end of the book, this is my prayer for the reader of this book.

"Now unto him that is able to keep you from falling, and to present you faultless before the presence of his glory with exceeding joy. To the only wise God our Savior, be glory and majesty, dominion and power, both now and ever. Amen." -Jude 24-25 (King James Version)

---

[2] Providing spiritual care - Marie Curie. Retrieved from https://www.mariecurie.org.uk/professionals/palliative-care-knowledge-zone/individual-needs/spirituality-end-life

Our Family 2020

Made in the USA
Middletown, DE
17 November 2021

52744672R00046